Let's Talk

Mark McArthur-Christie

OXFORD
UNIVERSITY PRESS

OXFORD
UNIVERSITY PRESS

Great Clarendon Street, Oxford OX2 6DP

Oxford University Press is a department of the University of Oxford.
It furthers the University's objective of excellence in research, scholarship,
and education by publishing worldwide in

Oxford   New York

Auckland   Bangkok   Buenos Aires   Cape Town   Chennai
Dar es Salaam   Delhi   Hong Kong   Istanbul   Karachi   Kolkata
Kuala Lumpur   Madrid   Melbourne   Mexico City   Mumbai   Nairobi
São Paulo   Shanghai   Singapore   Taipei   Tokyo   Toronto

with an associated company in Berlin

Oxford is a registered trade mark of Oxford University Press
in the UK and in certain other countries

© Mark McArthur-Christie 2002

The moral rights of the author have been asserted

Database right Oxford University Press (maker)

First published 2002

All rights reserved. No part of this publication may be reproduced,
stored in a retrieval system, or transmitted, in any form or by any means,
without the prior permission in writing of Oxford University Press,
or as expressly permitted by law, or under terms agreed with the appropriate
reprographics rights organization. Enquiries concerning reproduction
outside the scope of the above should be sent to the Rights Department,
Oxford University Press, at the address above

You must not circulate this book in any other binding or cover
and you must impose this same condition on any acquirer

British Library Cataloguing in Publication Data

Data available

ISBN 0 19 917516 0

10 9 8 7 6 5 4 3 2 1

Inspection Pack (nine different titles)   ISBN 0 19 917524 1
Guided Reading Pack (six of the same title)   ISBN 0 19 917841 0
Class Pack   ISBN 0 19 917525 X

Acknowledgements

The publisher would like to thank the following for permission to reproduce
photographs:

Corbis/Bob Mitchell p 1; Hulton Getty pp 5 (*top*), 10 (*top*), 14 (*top*), 16;
Mary Evans Picture Library p 12 (*left and right*); Popperfoto/Reuters/Toshiyuki
Aizwa p 14 (*bottom*); Science & Society pp 8, 9, 11 and back cover; Science
Photo Library/David Ducros p 19 (*bottom*), Science Photo Library/Alfred Pasieka
p 20 (*bottom*); Topham Picturepoint p 17 (*top*)

Illustrations by Francis Bacon pp 1, 5 (*bottom*), 13 (*top*), 15 (*bottom*) and back
cover, 19 (*top*), 20 (*top*), 21; Stefan Chabluk p18; Bill Donohoe pp 3, 4, 6, 7, 10
(*bottom*), 13 (*bottom*), 15 (*top*), 17 (*bottom*), 22–23

Front cover photograph © Patrick Shéandell O'Carroll/PhotoAlto

Printed in Hong Kong

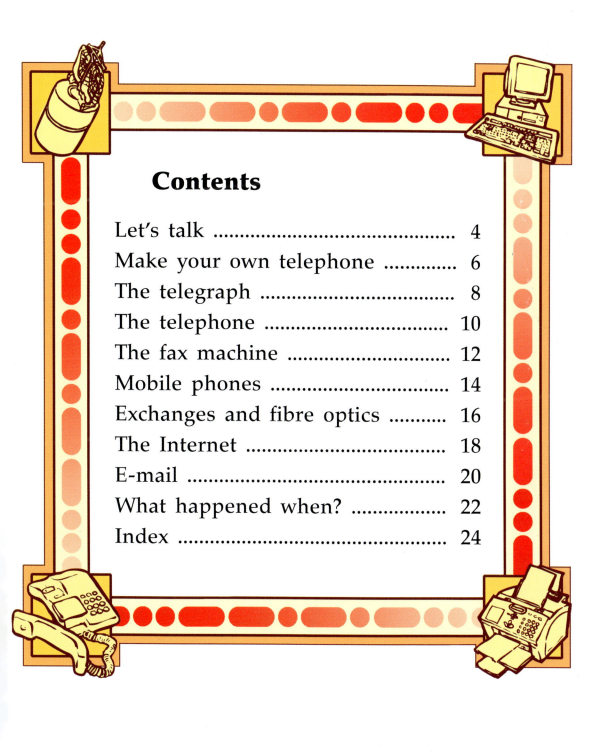

Contents

Let's talk 4
Make your own telephone 6
The telegraph 8
The telephone 10
The fax machine 12
Mobile phones 14
Exchanges and fibre optics 16
The Internet 18
E-mail 20
What happened when? 22
Index 24

Let's talk

People have always needed to communicate with each other. If people are close enough to see and hear each other, they can talk. If they are far apart it is more difficult. The way we communicate over distance is changing all the time.

Two hundred years ago, if you wanted to communicate with someone far away you had to send a letter. It could take months.

The first letters were carried by messengers on horseback.

One hundred years ago, you could talk to someone hundreds of miles away by telephone.

Today, we can communicate with people all over the world in lots of different ways. We can talk on mobile phones, send faxes, read text messages and send e-mails. As well as using words, we can send moving pictures, sounds, and music.

Making a telephone call in 1910

FACT BOX

All types of communication need: a sender, a receiver, a message, and a medium.

Make your own telephone

Telephones carry our voices to people who are too far away to hear them normally.

You can make a very simple telephone. It works by sending vibrations from your voice along a piece of string.

FACT BOX

The word "telephone" comes from two Greek words:

"tele" means "far away", "phone" means "sound".

You will need:

- 2 clean, empty cans (with no sharp edges) or hard plastic cups
- a long piece of string
- a thin nail and hammer
- a partner
- an adult to help

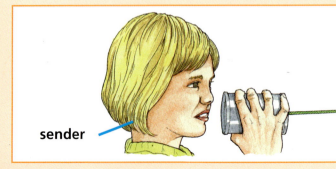

sender

Step 1

Ask the adult to make a small hole in the bottom of each can.

Step 2

Thread the string through the holes. Tie a knot in the string at each end.

Step 3

Ask your partner to hold one can to his or her ear. Stretch the string until it is tight. Speak into your can, and your partner should be able to hear you. Swap over.

The string vibrates, carrying the message.

receiver

The telegraph

In 1836, Samuel Morse, an American, joined two metal keys with wire which carried electricity. If he tapped one key, the electricity made the other key move at the same time. He could send messages a long way using a long wire.

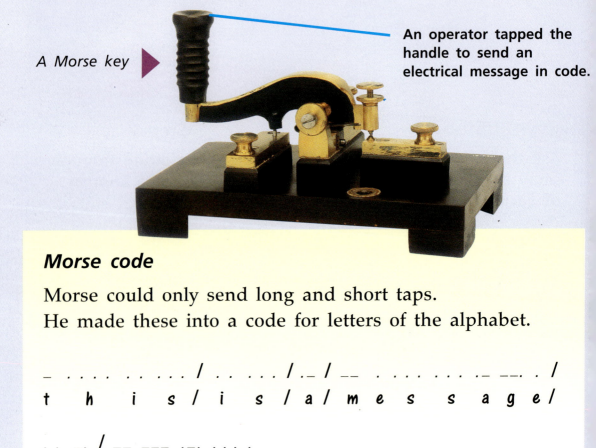

A Morse key ▶

An operator tapped the handle to send an electrical message in code.

Morse code

Morse could only send long and short taps.
He made these into a code for letters of the alphabet.

_ . . . . / . . . . . / ._ / __ . . . . . . ._ __. . /
t   h   i   s / i   s / a / m e   s   a g e /

. . _. / __ ___ ._. . . . .
i n / M o   r   s e

Morse telegraphs were used at railway stations to send messages about trains.

FACT BOX

The word "telegraph" comes from two Greek words:
 "tele" means "far away",
 "graph" means "writing".

In 1837, in England, William Cooke and Charles Wheatstone made another type of telegraph. It used electricity to move iron needles. The needles pointed to letters and numbers on a wooden board.

Cooke and Wheatstone's telegraph ▶

letters

moving needles

keys

The telephone

Alexander Graham Bell was a teacher of deaf children. He worked out how electricity could carry the human voice. In 1876, Bell invented the telephone. People could now talk directly to each other, even if they were some distance apart.

Alexander Graham Bell with his invention – the telephone – in 1892.

How it works

When you speak into a telephone, a transmitter turns your words into electrical signals. These signals travel down the telephone wire to the receiver.

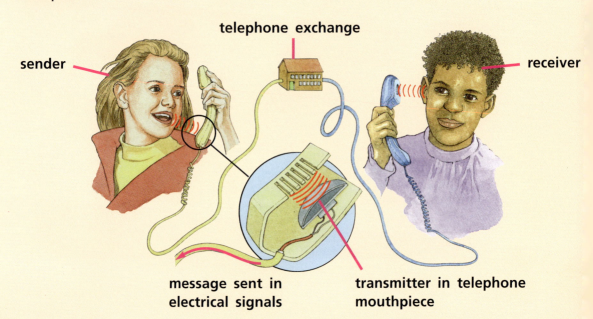

Telephones have changed in style over the years, but they still work in a similar way.

1877

1881

1890

1905

1930

1992

11

The fax machine

The next big step in communication over distance was sending pictures.

In 1907, German inventor Arthur Korn used telephone wires to send simple pictures between Munich and Berlin. The pictures were not very clear.

Edouard Belin invented the first machine that could send good quality pictures in 1913. It was called a Belinograph.

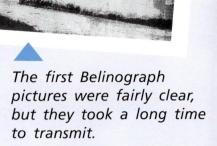

The first Belinograph pictures were fairly clear, but they took a long time to transmit.

At an exhibition in Paris, Belin showed how his new machine could send pictures over a distance.

People who made newspapers used fax machines to get photographs from journalists abroad. Speed was important, to keep the news up to date. However, early faxes were slow compared to modern faxes.

A newspaper office with a fax machine in the 1950s

How it works

A fax works by scanning little bits of a picture at a time. These bits are sent down a telephone wire as pulses of electricity. The receiver fax converts the electrical pulses and prints the picture bit by bit.

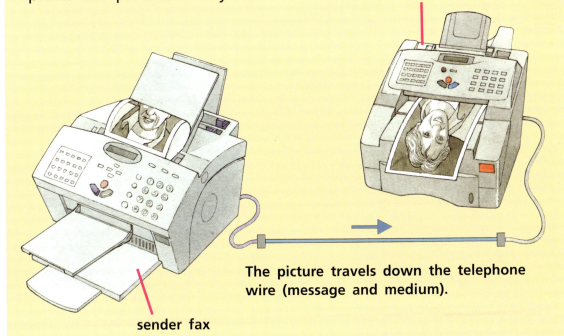

receiver fax

sender fax

The picture travels down the telephone wire (message and medium).

Mobile phones

The first mobile telephones were big and heavy. They were built into cars.

By the 1970s, mobile phones were smaller so people could carry them around. They were still big compared to modern mobile phones.

A 1970s mobile phone had a bulky transmitter pack as well as a handset.

handset

transmitter pack

A mobile phone in 2001

FACT BOX

In the 1970s, lots of people wanted mobile phones but there were not enough telephone lines for everyone. By 1976, waiting lists for mobiles were ten years long!

Modern mobiles work by sending a signal to the nearest transmitter mast. The area the mast covers is called a "cell". The mast beams the call onto the next cell. Most wealthy countries are covered by cells, so you can make calls all over the world.

Transmitter masts beam calls onto the next cell.

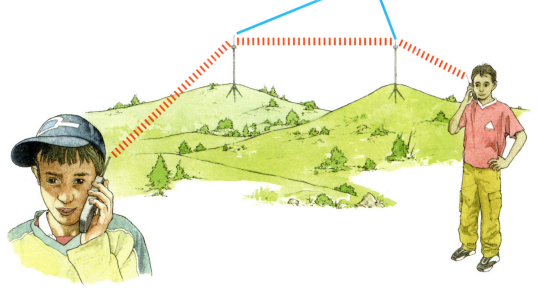

On most modern mobiles you can send text as well as speech. Some people use a special code with a mix of words and numbers.

This message says "See you later".

Exchanges and fibre optics

In 1877, the first telephones were sold and the first telephone exchange opened. This meant that lots of different people could talk to each other – as long as they all had telephones!

At the exchange, operators moved electrical plugs on a board to connect calls.

As telephones became more popular, the copper wires that carried the calls became overloaded.

In 1970, American scientists discovered that ultra-pure glass could be made into long, fine threads. The threads (fibre-optic cables) could carry up to 40,000 telephone calls at a time.

copper cable

fibre-optic cable

How it works

In fibre-optic cables, the sender's words are changed to on/off pulses of light by an encoder. These pulses travel down the cable. The light signals are turned into words again at the other end by a decoder and the receiver hears the voice.

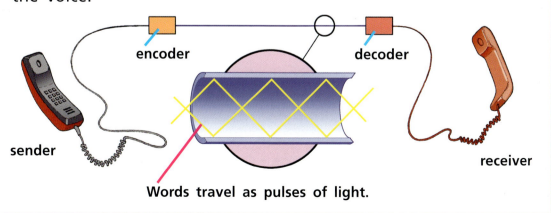

encoder

decoder

sender

receiver

Words travel as pulses of light.

The Internet

The Internet is a huge source of information. It is like lots of libraries linked together, but as well as text, it has sounds and moving pictures.

The Internet is also a massive centre for communication. The way into the Internet is through your computer.

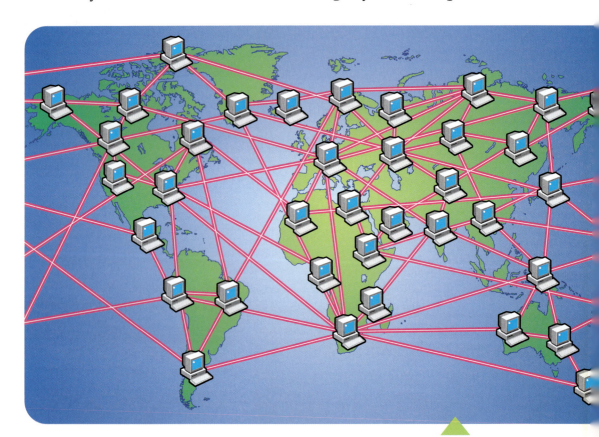

Today there are more than 1.6 billion people using the Internet.

FACT BOX

There are nearly 30 billion web pages on the Internet. Web pages are like book pages, but you can make things change on screen by using a mouse.

How did the Internet begin?

The Internet began in 1969 when the American government and military researchers linked their computers together. This meant they could see and share the same information quickly and safely.

In the 1970s most computer screens were green. Floppy disks were 13cm (5.25 inches) square.

Soon other researchers began to use the network, and in just a few years the network of computers grew. Now it spreads across the world and even into space!

Satellites relay computer data, telephone and fax messages, as well as TV signals.

E-mail

One of the first main uses of the Internet was sending text e-mails. Now people can send pictures, sounds and even moving images by e-mail.

Binary code

Computers change all the information they use into 1s and 0s. This is called "binary code". The computer sends millions of these 1s and 0s around its circuits as on/off pulses of electricity. It uses a special circuit called a "central processing unit" (CPU) to turn the pulses into pictures and words on the screen.

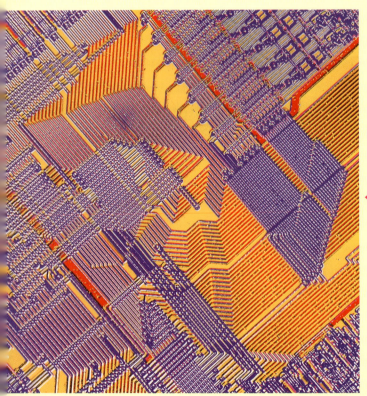

◀ This photo (taken with a special camera) shows the surface of a computer chip. You can see some of the circuits which carry the electrical pulses.

How it works

To send a message, your computer turns what you have written into binary code. It sends it down a telephone line using a modem. At the other end, another modem unscrambles the signals and shows the message on a computer screen.

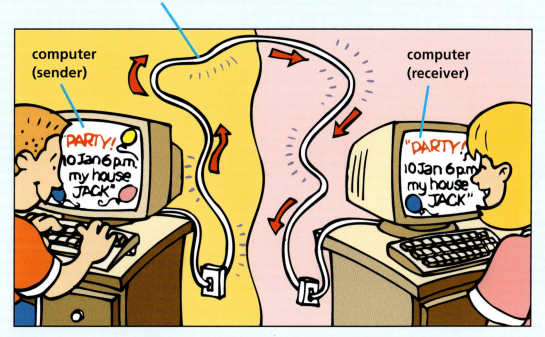

The message travels down telephone lines.

Communication is getting faster

Modern modems can send messages 50 times faster than modems in the 1960s. ISDN telephone lines can send messages 100 times faster than ordinary telephone lines!

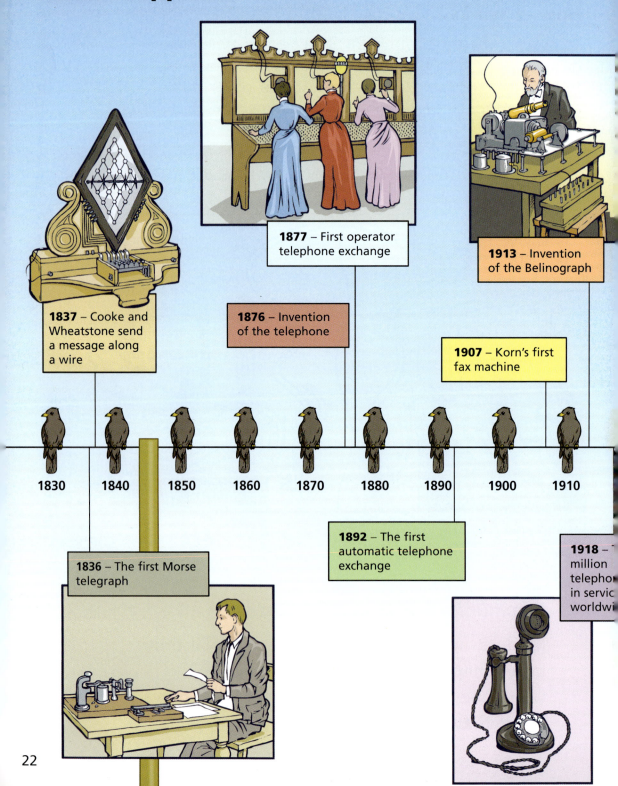

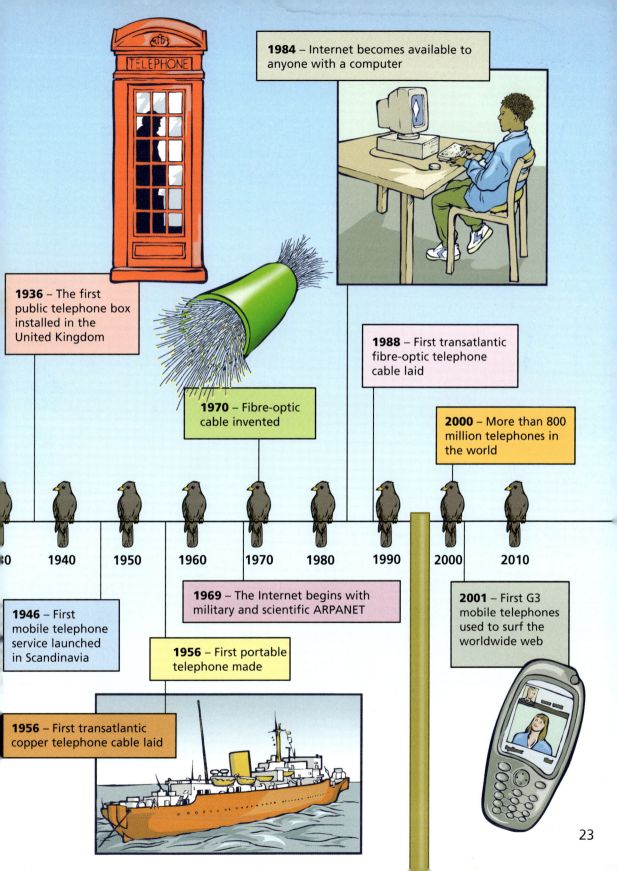

Index

Belin Edouard 12
Belinograph 12, 22
Bell, Alexander 10
binary code 20, 21
cable, copper 17, 23
cable, fibre-optic 17, 23
computer 18–21, 23
Cooke, William 9, 22
CPU 20
e-mail 20, 5
exchange 16, 22
faxes 5, 12–13, 22
Internet 18–21, 23
Korn, Arthur 12
letter 4
messenger 4
mobile phones 5, 14–15, 23
modem 21
Morse code 8, 22
Morse, Samuel 8
satellites 19
telegraph 8–9, 22
telephone 5, 6–7, 10–11, 14–17, 19, 21, 22, 23
text messages 15
web pages 18
Wheatstone, Charles 9, 22

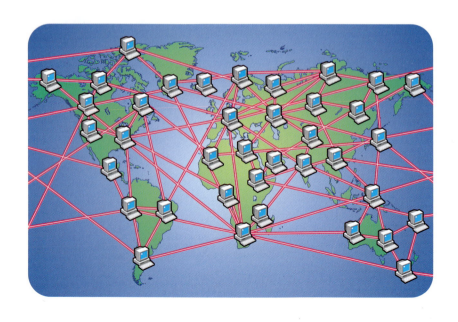